Vocabulary Booster
for Cambridge English Qualifications

A2 FLYERS

How to use this book

Introduction

Team Together Vocabulary Boosters are designed to be a fun and engaging way of consolidating and extending vocabulary from the *Team Together* series. Each Vocabulary Booster includes 10 units, based around a different topic relevant to children and their lives. The books also offer support for children preparing for the Cambridge English Qualifications for young learners.

Vocabulary presentation

In the first part of each unit, key vocabulary is introduced in the context of a large, colourful scene, which will engage children and spark their curiosity. Children are encouraged to explore the scene through a series of short activities and accompanying audio.

Labels for key vocabulary.

Audio and exercises present the language in context.

Fun facts boxes give children additional information about the topic. Remember! boxes give tips on language, e.g. irregular English spelling patterns.

Additional questions encourage children to explore the scene further.

Children find Frank hiding in each scene.

Vocabulary practice

In the second part of each unit, there are two pages of activities which provide further consolidation and practice of the vocabulary through a variety of fun activities.

Target icons identify Cambridge English Qualifications style tasks.

Vocabulary practised through reading and listening tasks.

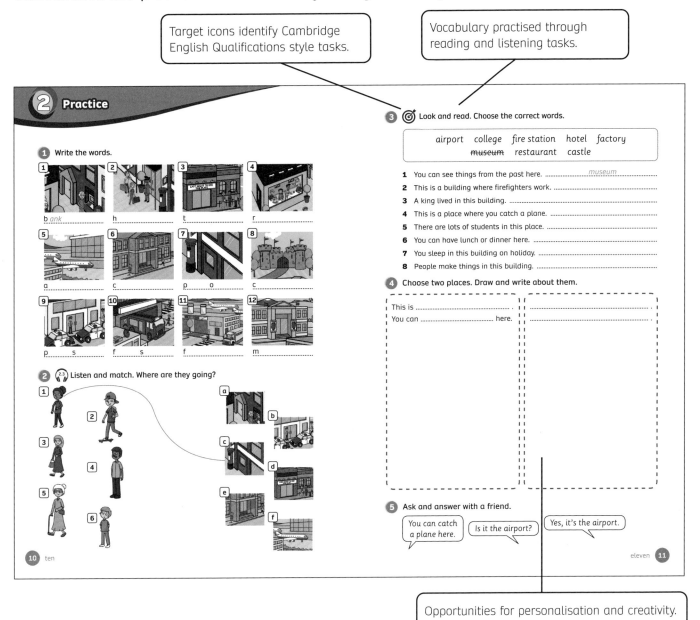

Opportunities for personalisation and creativity.

Other books in the series

There are three Vocabulary Booster books in the *Team Together* series, each one relating to one of the Cambridge English Qualifications for young learners tests:

- Pre A1 Starters

- A1 Movers

- A2 Flyers

We suggest that you use the Vocabulary Booster for Cambridge English Qualifications A2 Flyers with *Team Together* Level 5.

Our final tip for using this book? Have fun!

1 At the stadium

flag

whistle

stripe

winner

silver

gold

prize

stadium

team

race

spot

photographer

1 🎧 **1.1** Listen and point. Repeat the words.

2 🎧 **1.2** Listen and number.

3 **Look and find someone who is ...**

1 wearing a jacket with yellow stripes.

2 wearing a skirt with purple spots.

3 waving an orange flag.

4 riding a blue bike.

5 eating an apple.

4 **Count. How many ... are there in the stadium?**

1 flags with silver spots

2 flags with gold stripes

3 people whistling

4 photographers

Fun fact

The biggest stadium in the world is in North Korea. How many people do you think it can hold?

Where's Frank?

① Practice

1 **Read the words and number the pictures.**

1 stadium
2 winner
3 prize
4 team
5 photographer
6 race
7 whistle
8 spot
9 stripe
10 flag
11 gold
12 silver

2 🎯 🎧 (1.3) **Listen and write.**

1 Going to watch: ....*athletics*............

2 Taking place at: Big City ....

3 Going to watch: six ....

4 Favourite team has: gold ....

5 The winner gets: a .... medal

3 🎯 🎧 (1.4) Read and circle the correct words. Then listen and check.

Welcome to the Big City ¹**Centre / Stadium.** We're going to watch some exciting ²**flags / races** this afternoon. There are two ³**teams / photographers** taking part. The first team are the Red Striped Runners. They've got red ⁴**spots / stripes** on their T-shirts. The other team are the Super Spotted Greens. They're wearing green T-shirts with white ⁵**stripes / spots**. There are lots of people in the stadium. They're all waving ⁶**prizes / flags** and cheering their team. The ⁷**photographers / silver** are taking pictures of the teams before the race.

The Red Stripes are running fast. The people in the stadium are ⁸**whistling / running** loudly.

The Red Stripes finish first. They're the ⁹**gold / winners**! The winners will get a ¹⁰**prize / whistle**! What a great day!

4 Answer for you.

1 How many team sports do you know? ....

2 Do you play any team sports? ....

3 Have you ever been to a big stadium?
   What did you do / see there? ....

4 Have you ever won a race or a prize?
   When? What was it? ....

5 Would you prefer to be a photographer or an
   athlete? Why? ....

5 Ask and answer with a friend.

How many team sports do you know?

Basketball, football ...

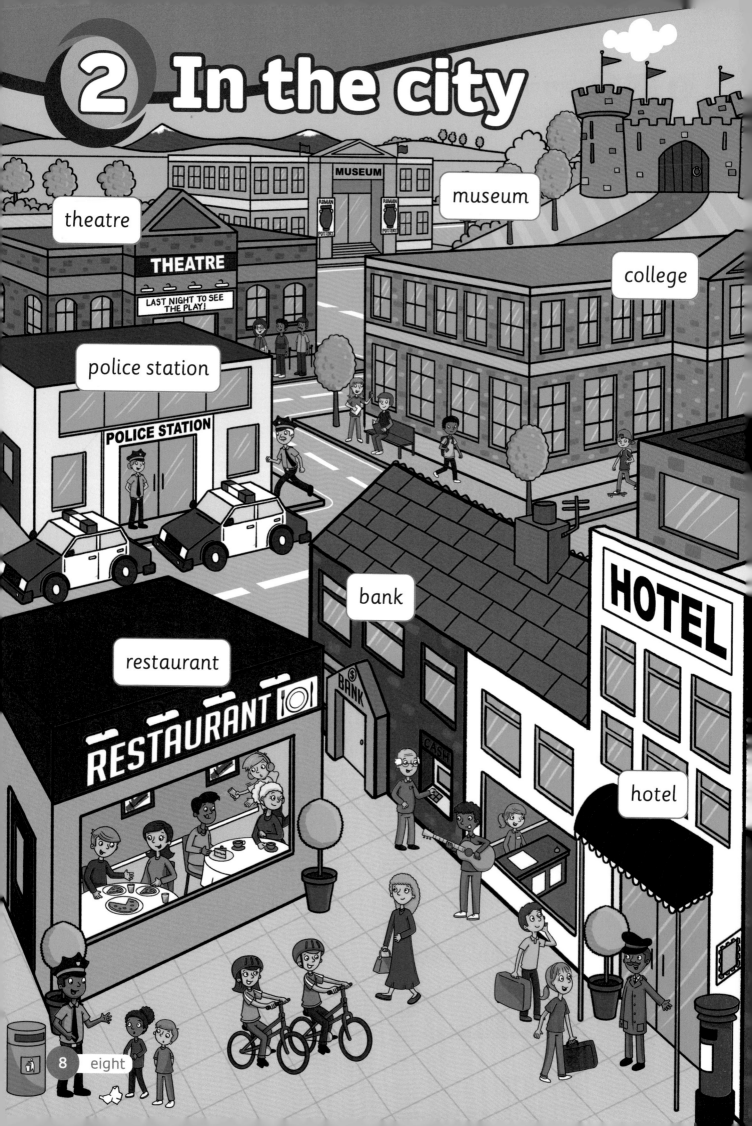

2 In the city

theatre

museum

college

police station

bank

restaurant

hotel

castle

airport

factory

HEALTHY FOODS

fire station

FIRE STATION

HEALTHY FOODS

BUS STOP

post office

OST OFFICE

1 🎧 2.1 Listen and point. Repeat the words.

2 🎧 2.2 Listen and say the place.

3 Look and find.

   1 a man driving a lorry.

   2 a firefighter wearing a yellow hat.

   3 a girl riding a bike.

   4 a student reading a red book.

   5 a boy waiting at the bus stop.

4 Close your book. Say all the places in the town that you can remember.

Fun fact

Singapore's Changi airport has a butterfly garden. It has more than 1000 butterflies!

Where's Frank?

nine **9**

1 Write the words.

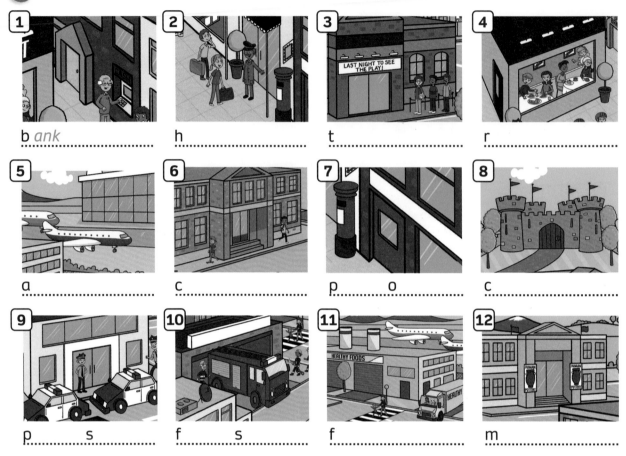

1 b *ank*

2 h

3 t

4 r

5 a

6 c

7 p o

8 c

9 p s

10 f s

11 f

12 m

2 (2.3) Listen and match. Where are they going?

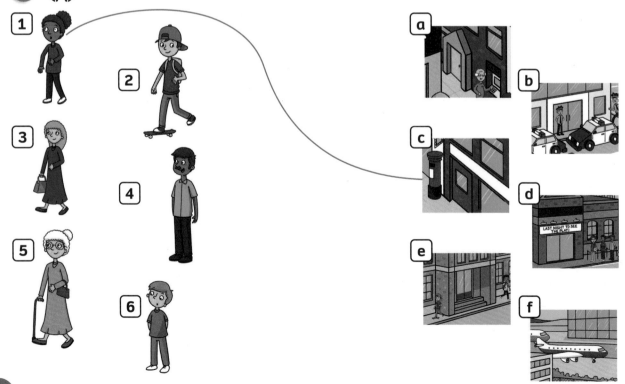

3 🎯 Look and read. Choose the correct words.

> airport   college   fire station   hotel   factory
> ~~museum~~   restaurant   castle

1 You can see things from the past here. ....*museum*...............

2 This is a building where firefighters work. ....

3 A king lived in this building. ....

4 This is a place where you catch a plane. ....

5 There are lots of students in this place. ....

6 You can have lunch or dinner here. ....

7 You sleep in this building on holiday. ....

8 People make things in this building. ....

4 Choose two places. Draw and write about them.

This is ....
You can .... here.

....
....

5 Ask and answer with a friend.

You can catch a plane here.

Is it the airport?

Yes, it's the airport.

3 It's time for breakfast

sugar

knife

spoon

jam

honey

fork

yoghurt

butter

cushion

cereal

salt   pepper

1 🎧 3.1 Listen and point. Repeat the words.

2 🎧 3.2 Listen and circle. Who is it?

3 Find someone who is ....

1 drinking a chocolate milkshake.

2 putting sugar in their coffee.

3 putting salt on their eggs.

4 reading an e-book.

5 wearing a jacket with red stripes.

4 How many ... can you see?

1 forks ☐

2 spoons ☐

3 knives ☐

4 cushions ☐

5 salt pots ☐

6 pepper pots ☐

Fun fact

Honey is 80% sugar!
What other foods
have a lot of sugar
in them?

Where's Frank?

1 Write the letters in the correct order. Then match the words and pictures.

1 a j m .... *jam*

2 r o k f ....

3 f i n e k ....

4 o n o p s ....

5 t u b e r t ....

6 e l a c r e ....

7 h i n o c u s ....

8 y o n e h ....

9 g u s a r ....

10 t h r o y u g ....

11 a l t s ....

12 p r e p e p ....

a

b

c

d

e S

f

g

h

i

j

k p

l

2 Read and choose the correct word.

1 You don't use this to cut things. You use it to eat soup. **spoon / knife**

2 This is something soft that you can sit on. **glass / cushion**

3 You put this on bread. It's soft and yellow. It's made from milk. **cereal / butter**

4 You find this in fruit, cakes and sweets. It's nice but we shouldn't eat too much. **yoghurt / sugar**

5 You can put it on bread. It's sweet and it's made from fruit. **jam / honey**

6 You can put this on your food. It comes from sea water. **fork / salt**

7 This is something sweet that's made by bees. **butter / honey**

3 (3.3) Listen and tick what you hear. Then complete the dialogue.

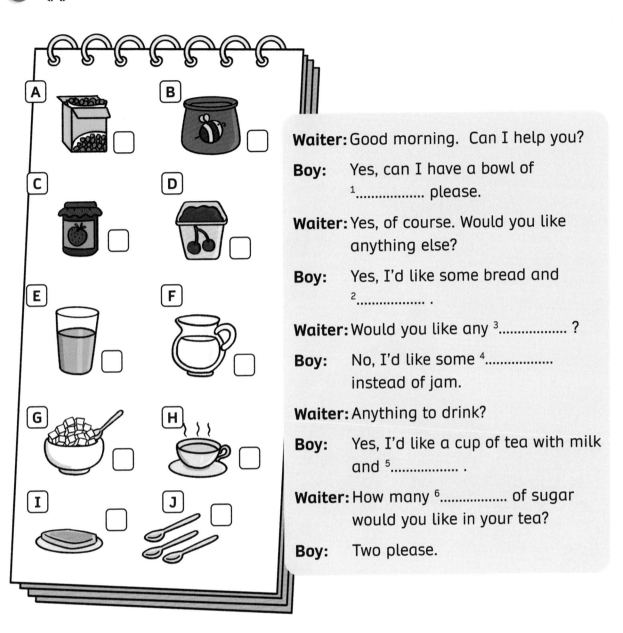

Waiter: Good morning. Can I help you?

Boy: Yes, can I have a bowl of 1................ please.

Waiter: Yes, of course. Would you like anything else?

Boy: Yes, I'd like some bread and 2................ .

Waiter: Would you like any 3................ ?

Boy: No, I'd like some 4................ instead of jam.

Waiter: Anything to drink?

Boy: Yes, I'd like a cup of tea with milk and 5................ .

Waiter: How many 6................ of sugar would you like in your tea?

Boy: Two please.

4 Answer the questions for you.

1 What do you eat for breakfast? ....

2 What do you use to eat your breakfast? ....

3 Do you put salt or pepper on your food? ....

4 Do you like yoghurt? What's your favourite kind? ....

5 How much sugar do you eat every day? ....

5 Ask and answer with a friend.

What do you eat for breakfast?

I have yoghurt and some fruit.

4 A camping trip

sore

bandage

elbow

look after

camp

fire

wood

torch

fetch

explore

tent

rucksack

1 **4.1** Listen and point. Repeat the words.

2 **4.2** Listen and chant. Then listen again and circle.

3 Find the animals in the wood.

1 a big, brown rabbit.

2 a small, black bat.

3 a blue and yellow bird.

4 a long green snake.

5 a big, yellow frog.

6 a small, red spider.

4 Close your books. Remember what food you can see in the picture.

Fun fact

There are some people in the world who still live in tents called 'yurts'. Can you find out who they are?

Where's Frank?

1 Find and circle. Then write.

camp

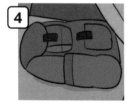

x	c	v	f	e	t	c	h	r	k	b
v	u	a	s	b	o	p	r	e	k	a
t	e	v	m	r	m	h	r	q	w	n
e	m	l	p	p	f	o	z	t	o	d
n	l	k	b	s	s	b	r	o	o	a
t	p	f	x	o	s	t	d	r	d	g
g	f	i	r	e	w	v	b	c	x	e
g	t	b	o	s	y	b	k	h	r	q
e	x	p	l	o	r	e	z	g	b	b
r	f	n	w	v	q	v	z	d	m	x
q	r	r	u	c	k	s	a	c	k	b

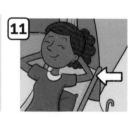

2 Read and circle the correct answer. You should…

1 keep your clothes in a **rucksack / cushion**.

2 take a **bandage / tent** to sleep in.

3 take a **camp / torch** to help you see in the dark.

4 cook your food on a **fire / wood**.

5 take a **sore / bandage** in case you cut yourself.

6 look **on / after** your friends and family on the camp.

7 **explore / fetch** and have fun!

3 🎯 Choose and write.

> explore   elbow   ~~camp~~   fire   bandage   sore   torch
> looking after   tents

Last weekend I went camping with my family. We found a place to

1 _camp_ next to a wood. We put up our 2................................ and put

our sleeping bags inside. Then I went to 3................................ the wood with

my brother Harry and my sister Holly. It was getting dark so we took a

4................................ . We were walking through the wood when Harry fell over

and hurt his arm. "Ouch! My 5................................ !" he shouted. "It's really

6................................ ." We went back to the camp and mum put a 7................................

on Harry's elbow. "Thank you for 8................................ Harry" she

said. Then we cooked dinner on the camp 9................................ . It was great fun!

4 Answer for you. Then choose one thing you've done. Draw and write.

Have you ever …

1 camped with your family or

friends? ....

2 slept in a tent? ....

3 explored a new place with

friends? ....

4 looked after a person or

animal? ....

5 worn a bandage?

....

5 Ask and answer with a friend.

> Have you ever
> been camping?

> Yes, I have. I went camping with
> the Countryside Club last year.

5 On stage

act

actor

friendly

unfriendly

bored

1

designer

costume

DRESSING ROOM

20 twenty

Betty Holly – **Concert**
June 30th

tune

concert

singer

stage

artist

1 **5.1** Listen and point. Repeat the words.

2 **5.2** Listen and number. Say the words.

3 Look and find.

1 a boy dancing at a concert.

2 a man playing a silver guitar.

3 a woman playing the drums.

4 a girl wearing gold shoes.

5 a man wearing a costume with stripes.

4 How many ... are there?

1 actors ☐

2 singers ☐

3 artists ☐

4 photographers ☐

Fun fact

In the past, the name 'actor' was only for men. A woman on the stage was called an 'actress'. But today the word 'actor' is used for both men and women.

Where's Frank?

1 Complete the puzzle. Find the mystery word.

1 Someone who is nice and likes talking to people is …

2 This is a group of musical notes that you sing. It's a …

3 Actors stand on this in a theatre. It's a …

4 Someone who draws or paints pictures is an …

5 Someone whose job is to sing is a …

6 A singer performs for people in a …

7 Someone who doesn't like talking to people is …

8 A person who works on TV or on the stage is an …

2 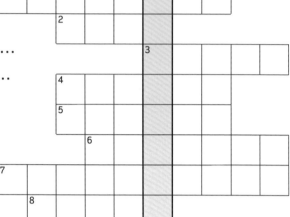 5.3 Listen and tick.

1 Who did David see at the weekend?

 A  B  C

2 How did David feel during the concert?

 A  B  C

3 Where did Emma go at the weekend?

 A  B  C

4 What was the best part of her evening?

 A  B   C

3 Complete the dialogues. Use the words in the box.

acted   singer   actor   artist   designer   friendly
tunes   ~~concert~~

Oliver: Have you ever been to a pop music ¹...*concert*... ?

Katy: Yes, I went to see my favourite ²................... Harry Frank, last month.

Oliver: Was he good?

Katy: Yes, he was great. His songs have really good ³............................... .

He was really nice too. He talked a lot and he was very ⁴................... .

Oliver: Have you ever been on the stage?

Katy: Yes, I ⁵............................... in the school play last year.

Oliver: Are you a good ⁶............................... ?

Katy: I'm not bad.

Oliver: Would you like to be an actor when you grow up?

Katy: No! I love clothes and fashion, so I'd like to be a clothes ⁷................... .

Oliver: I love drawing and painting. I'd like to be an ⁸............................... .
How about you?

4 Think and answer for you.

1 Who's your favourite singer / actor? ....

2 Have you ever been to a concert? ....

3 Can you act? Can you sing a tune? ....

4 When are you bored? ....

5 Which job would you choose: actor, designer, artist or singer?
Why? ....

5 Ask and answer with a friend.

Have you ever been to a concert?

Yes, I went to a pop concert last year.

Who did you see?

I saw my favourite singer …

Review 1

1 Circle the words. Then choose and write.

teamraceflagwinnerstadiumprizephotographerwhistle

1 Basketball and football are _t e a m_ sports.

2 A place where people watch sports is a __ __ __ __ __ __ __ .

3 Ten athletes ran in the __ __ __ __ .

4 Can you __ __ __ __ __ __ __ a tune?

5 A person who takes photos is a __ __ __ __ __ __ __ __ __ __ __ __ __ .

6 Every country has a national __ __ __ __ .

7 The first runner to finish the race is the __ __ __ __ __ __ .

8 The winner of a competition gets a __ __ __ __ __ .

2 Read and circle the correct answer.

1 I need to get some money from the …

bank   shopping centre   museum

2 When we went on holiday we stayed in a …

post office   airport   hotel

3 My dad is a firefighter. He works at the …

theatre   fire station   police station

4 My brother studies English at …

college   a restaurant   a hotel

5 People make things in a …

castle   factory   theatre

6 We're flying to Spain from the …

bus stop   train station   airport

3 Write the words. Label the picture.

1 k.*nife*

2 f.

3 s.

4 c.

5 s.

6 j.

7 h.

8 y.

9 b.

4 Find and circle six differences. Then read and write 1 or 2.

1 There's a camp fire. ....

2 The girl hasn't got a torch. ....

3 There are four rucksacks. ....

4 Mum's got a bandage. ....

5 The tents are blue. ....

6 The boy's got a sore elbow. ....

5 Write the words.

1 I'm not interested in this play.

I'm b.*ored*..................... .

2 I'm an actor.

I work in a theatre, on the

s............................ .

I can a............................ .

3 I'm a singer.

I often perform in

c............................ .

I can sing a t............................ .

4 I work with colours.

I'm good at drawing and

painting.

I'm an a ....

5 I work in the theatre.

I design clothes for actors.

I'm a c............................

d............................ .

6 I don't like talking to people.

I'm not friendly.

I'm u............................ .

6 A bicycle ride

cycle

BICYCLE REPAIRS

POST OFFICE

MARKET

wheel

repair

helmet

bicycle

tyre

stone

railway

hill

bridge

stream

pond

1 🎧6.1 **Listen and point. Repeat the words.**

2 🎧6.2 **Listen and number.**

3 **Look and find someone who …**

1 is riding a red bicycle.

2 is wearing a purple helmet with white spots.

3 is carrying a green rucksack.

4 has got a brown beard.

5 is wearing a black t-shirt.

4 **How many … are there?**

1 yellow ducklings on the pond

2 orange fish in the stream

3 blue birds in the sky

4 silver bicycles

Fun fact

The most famous cycling race in the world is the Tour de France. Riders cycle over 2000 miles in 23 days! Do you know where the race finishes?

Where's Frank?

twenty-seven 27

6 Practice

1 Look and write the words.

1. h *ill* ....
2. p ....
3. s ....
4. b ....

5. s ....
6. h ....
7. r ....
8. b ....

9. w ....
10. t ....
11. c ....
12. r ....

2 Read and match.

1. It's a small piece of rock.
2. You must wear this on your head when you're cycling.
3. You can climb it.
   It's a small mountain.
4. It's a small piece of water.
   Ducks like to swim on it.
5. You cross it to go over a river or stream.
6. It's made of metal.
   Trains run along it.
7. You do this if something is broken.
8. It's part of a bicycle wheel.
   It has air in it.

a. railway
b. pond
c. repair
d. stone
e. bridge
f. tyre
g. helmet
h. hill

3 🎯 Choose the right words and write them on the lines.

Last week I got a new ¹ *bicycle*. The next day I went ² .... with my friend, George. We put on our ³ .... and rode our bikes into the countryside. Then we went over the ⁴ .... and up the ⁵ .... Suddenly, the front ⁶ .... of my bicycle hit a big ⁷ .... on the path. All the air came out of the ⁸ .... and I couldn't ride my bike any more. Luckily, there was a shop nearby. We took my bicycle there and the kind man ⁹ .... it for me. Then I ¹⁰ .... home happily.

1	wheel	bicycle	tyre
2	cycle	cycled	cycling
3	wheels	helmets	tyres
4	wheel	tyre	bridge
5	hill	pond	cycle

6	wheel	repair	railway
7	stream	stone	pond
8	pond	stream	tyre
9	cycle	repair	repaired
10	bicycle	cycled	cycle

4 Answer for you. Then draw and write about one answer.

1 Can you ride a bicycle? ....

2 Is it better to cycle in the city or in the countryside? Why? ....

3 Do you like travelling on the railway? ....

4 Have you ever climbed up a big hill? ....

5 Have you ever repaired something? What? ....

6 Are there any bridges in your town? ....

5 Ask and answer with a friend.

Do you go cycling at the weekend?

Yes, I cycle to school every day.

7 At the office

engineer

skyscraper

journalist

meeting

businessman

newspaper

businesswoman

entrance

exit

ENTRANCE ⬆ **EXIT** ⬇

NEWS

DAILY NEWS
FAMOUS ACTOR
OLIVER GEORGE
WINS PRIZE!

TOOLS

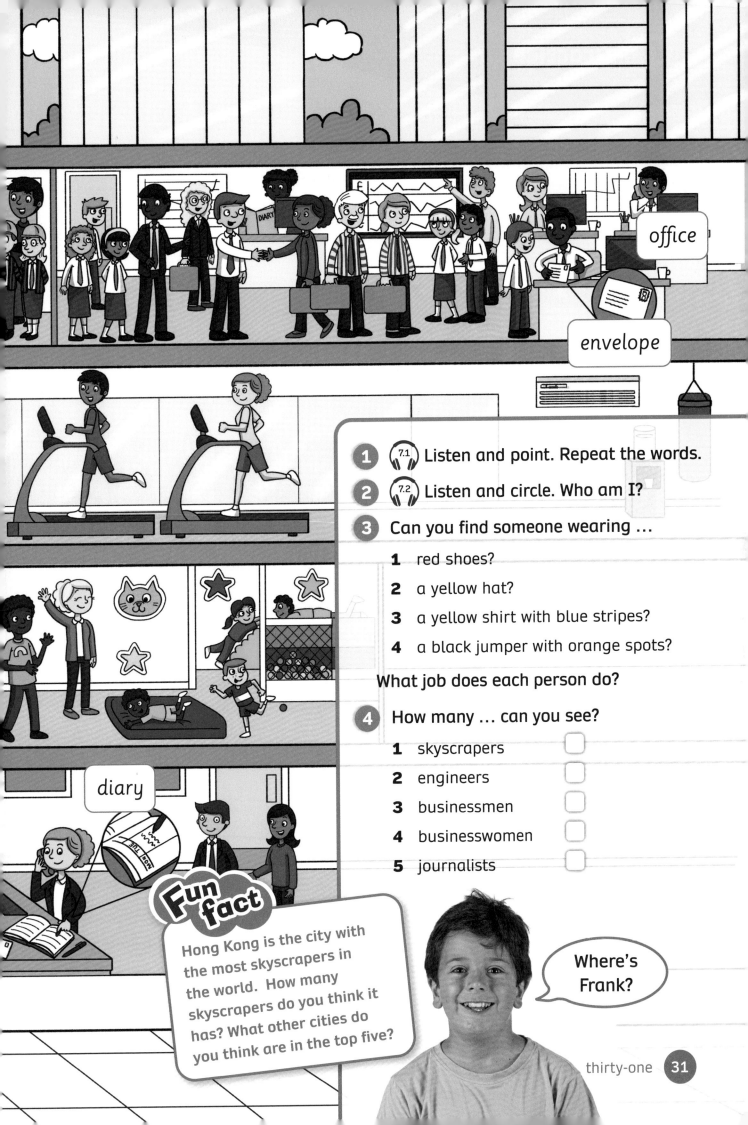

office

envelope

1 **7.1** Listen and point. Repeat the words.

2 **7.2** Listen and circle. Who am I?

3 Can you find someone wearing ...

1 red shoes?

2 a yellow hat?

3 a yellow shirt with blue stripes?

4 a black jumper with orange spots?

What job does each person do?

4 How many ... can you see?

1 skyscrapers

2 engineers

3 businessmen

4 businesswomen

5 journalists

diary

Fun fact

Hong Kong is the city with the most skyscrapers in the world. How many skyscrapers do you think it has? What other cities do you think are in the top five?

Where's Frank?

1 Choose and write the words.

> entrance ~~exit~~ engineer journalist office newspaper
> meeting diary skyscraper envelope businessman businesswoman

exit

....

....

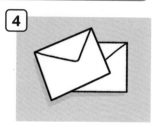

....

....

....

....

....

....

....

....

2 (7.3) Listen. Then circle the correct answers.

1 Sarah's mum works in — **a** a hospital — **b** an office.
2 She writes for a — **a** college — **b** newspaper.
3 Sarah's mum is a — **a** businesswoman — **b** journalist.
4 Her office is on the top floor of a — **a** skyscraper — **b** factory.
5 Sarah's dad is — **a** a businessman — **b** an engineer.
6 He has to go to lots of — **a** banks — **b** meetings.
7 Sarah likes working with — **a** people — **b** machines.
8 She wants to be — **a** an engineer — **b** a journalist.

3 Read the definitions. Write the words.

1 Something you read to find out the news. .... *newspaper* ....

2 A very tall building. ....

3 Someone who designs and builds machines. ....

4 When a group of people talk about work and make decisions. ....

5 A book for writing dates and meetings in. ....

6 The door you use to go into a building. ....

7 Something you put a letter in before you post it. ....

8 A place where businessmen and businesswomen work. ....

4 Can you write the definitions for these words?

1 journalist ....

2 businessman ....

3 exit ....

4 businesswoman ....

5 skyscraper ....

5 Answer the questions for you.

1 Do you know anyone who works in an office? ....

2 Do you keep a diary? ....

3 Have you ever been to the top of a skyscraper? ....

4 Would you like to be a businessman / woman? Why / Why not? ....

5 Would you prefer to be an engineer or a journalist? Why? ....

6 Does anyone in your family read a newspaper? ....

6 Now ask a friend the questions from activity 5.
Tell them your answers.

Do you know anyone who works in an office?

Yes, my mum works in an office. She's a ...

8 At school

surname

language

dictionary

science

geography

history

maths

gym

shelf

member

student

art

DO YOU WANT TO BE A MEMBER? Come and Join us!

1

Miss Brown.

Can you sing? Become a member of the School Band!

MATHS CLUB

ART CLUB

MUSIC CLUB

1 (8.1) **Listen and point. Repeat the words.**

2 (8.2) **Listen and say the chant.**

3 **Find the teachers with these surnames. What do they teach?**

1 Miss Brown. ....

2 Mr Johnson. ....

3 Mrs Smith. ....

4 Mr Evans. ....

4 **How many ... are there?**

1 boys in the geography classroom

2 girls in the science lab

3 teachers in the gym

4 students in the chess club

5 members in the school band

Fun fact

The three most spoken languages in the world are Mandarin, Spanish and English. Can you find out where people speak these languages?

Where's Frank?

1 Find and circle. Write the words.

1

.... *art* ....

5

....

6

....

7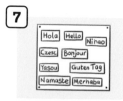

....

2

....

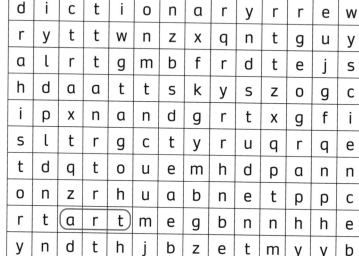

d	i	c	t	i	o	n	a	r	y	r	r	e	w
r	y	t	t	w	n	z	x	q	n	t	g	u	y
a	l	r	t	g	m	b	f	r	d	t	e	j	s
h	d	a	a	t	s	k	y	s	z	o	g	c	
i	p	x	n	a	d	g	r	t	x	g	f	i	
s	l	t	r	g	c	t	y	r	u	q	r	q	e
t	d	q	t	o	u	e	m	h	d	p	a	n	n
o	n	z	r	h	u	a	b	n	e	t	p	p	c
r	t	a	r	t	m	e	g	b	n	n	h	h	e
y	n	d	t	h	j	b	z	e	t	m	y	y	b
r	q	u	r	m	a	n	e	y	n	t	w	t	b
q	d	f	f	q	v	v	k	g	g	d	d	n	m
w	m	a	t	h	s	x	z	z	s	h	e	l	f

8

....

3

....

10

....

4

....

11

....

2 🎯 🎧 (8.3) Listen and write.

Student Information Card

1 Student's first name: .... *David* ....

2 Surname: ....

3 Going to study: Science, Maths and ....

4 Lunchtime activity in the: ....

5 Member of: .... club

3 Choose and write.

> dictionary   surname   member   languages   ~~history~~
> maths   students   shelf

1 I want to learn about kings and queens in the past. I'd like to study ....*history*.......... .

2 I like learning English and Spanish, or Chinese! I'm good at ....

3 I'm not very good with numbers. I don't like ....

4 I keep all my books on a .... in my bedroom.

5 There are 25 .... in each class at our school.

6 What's your science teacher's .... ? It's Evans. Mrs Evans.

7 I'm a .... of the chess club. We meet every day at 4 pm.

8 If I don't know what a word means, I look it up in the ....

4 Draw and write about yourself and your school.

My first name is: ....

My surname is: ....

At school I study .... ,

.... and ....

My favourite subject is ....

because ....

I'm a member of ....

5 Ask and answer with a friend.

What's your surname?

It's ...

Are you a member of any clubs?

Yes, I'm a member of ...

9 Our environment

fur

eagle

swan

creature

tortoise

beetle

spotted

insect

wing

nest

butterfly

wild

1 🎧 9.1 **Listen and point. Repeat the words.**

2 🎧 9.2 **Listen and chant.**

3 **Find someone who is ...**

1 taking a photo of a butterfly.

2 picking up a plastic bottle.

3 collecting insects.

4 watching an eagle.

4 **How many ... are there in the picture?**

1 purple beetles ☐

2 spotted butterflies ☐

3 eagles ☐

4 tortoises ☐

5 baby swans ☐

Fun fact

Butterflies don't taste with their mouths – they taste with their feet!

Where's Frank?

1 Reorder the letters. Number the pictures.

1 r u f .... *fur* ....

2 e b e t e l ....

3 n a w s ....

4 r o s e t o t i ....

5 f l u t t e r b y ....

6 g w i n ....

7 t e n s ....

8 r a t u c r e e ....

9 g a l e e ....

10 d e t t o p s ....

2 Read. Write the words.

1 This animal can run and jump. It's got black, brown or white fur.
It's got long ears. It's a .... *rabbit* ....

2 This creature eats plants. It's got four legs but it moves slowly.
It's got a hard shell. It's a ....

3 This bird has got big wings and it can fly very quickly.
It eats small creatures like insects and mice. It's an ....

4 This bird lives on the water. It has wings, but it doesn't often fly.
It's got a long white neck. It's a ....

5 These insects are beautiful. They have different colours and patterns
on their wings. Sometimes they are spotted. They're ....

6 This insect is often black, but can be green or other colours.
It's got two sets of wings and a hard shell. It's a ....

3 🎯 🎧(9.3) Listen and colour.

4 Finish colouring the picture. Then show your picture to a friend.

5 Can you answer the questions? Tick which of these:

1 ... creatures are insects?
- [ ] butterflies
- [ ] beetles
- [ ] eagles

2 ... creatures have wings?
- [ ] tortoises
- [ ] beetles
- [ ] swans

3 ... creatures have fur?
- [ ] butterflies
- [ ] rabbits
- [ ] beetles

4 ... is a wild animal?
- [ ] a pet tortoise
- [ ] a pet rabbit
- [ ] an eagle

10 A holiday in Egypt

pyramid

1

pyjamas

2

sunglasses

shampoo

postcard   comb

suitcase

trainers

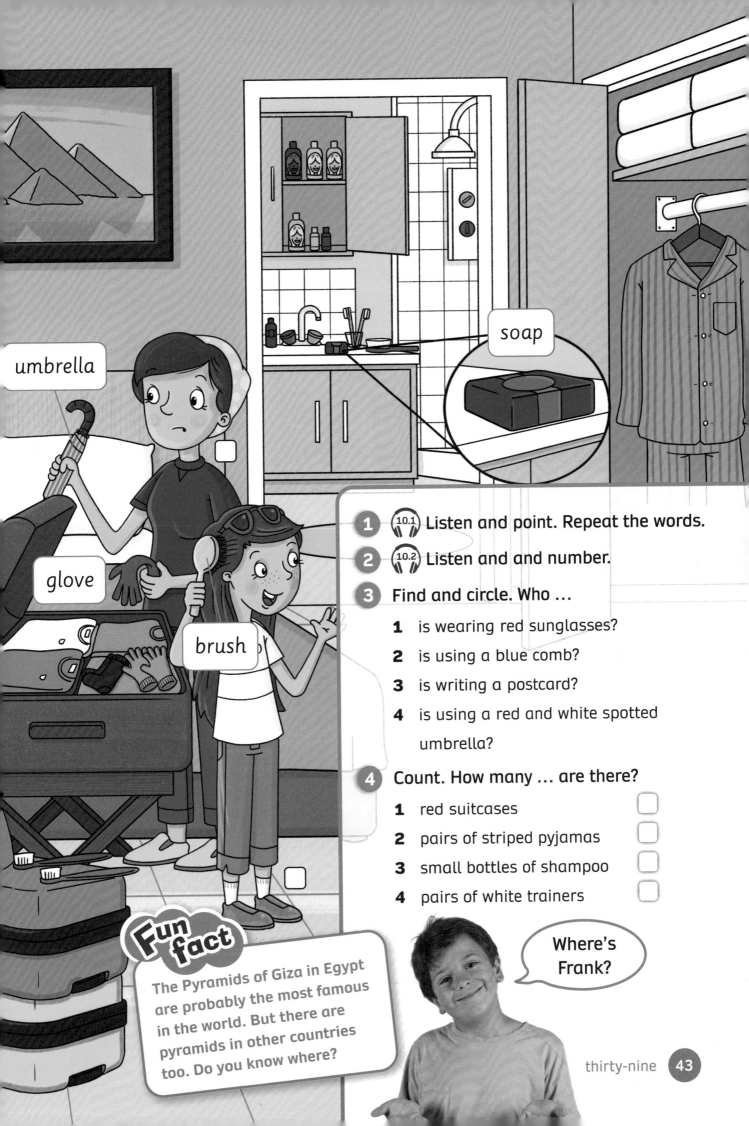

umbrella

glove

brush

soap

1 (10.1) Listen and point. Repeat the words.

2 (10.2) Listen and and number.

3 Find and circle. Who ...

1 is wearing red sunglasses?

2 is using a blue comb?

3 is writing a postcard?

4 is using a red and white spotted umbrella?

4 Count. How many ... are there?

1 red suitcases

2 pairs of striped pyjamas

3 small bottles of shampoo

4 pairs of white trainers

Fun fact

The Pyramids of Giza in Egypt are probably the most famous in the world. But there are pyramids in other countries too. Do you know where?

Where's Frank?

1 Write the words.

1 brush
2 ....
3 ....
4 ....

5 ....
6 ....
7 ....
8 ....

9 ....
10 ....
11 ....
12 ....

2 🎧 10.3 What does Katy pack in her suitcase? Listen and tick.

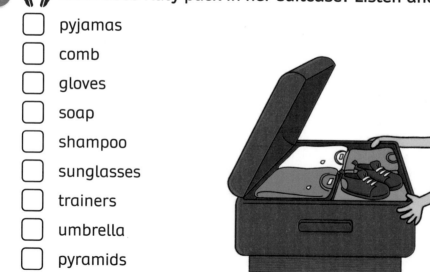

☐ pyjamas
☐ comb
☐ gloves
☐ soap
☐ shampoo
☐ sunglasses
☐ trainers
☐ umbrella
☐ pyramids

3 Choose and write the words.

Dear Oliver

I'm writing this [1]............................. from Egypt! We're having a nice time now,
but when we first arrived our [2]............................. got lost at the airport.
For two days we didn't have any of our things. We didn't have any
[3]............................. so we couldn't have a shower! And I didn't have my
bottle of [4]............................. or my [5]............................. so I couldn't
wash or comb my hair! Luckily I didn't lose my [6].............................
The sun is so bright here that you can't go out without wearing them.
We went to visit the famous [7]............................. yesterday.
They were amazing. We did a lot of walking so I'm happy
that I've got my comfortable [8]............................. to wear.
I brought an [9]............................. , but I won't need it
as it's really hot and dry here.

Lots of love

Sarah

shampoo   sunglasses   postcard   trainers   umbrella   pyramids   soap   comb   suitcases

4 Where would you like to go on holiday? Draw and write about what you'll take in your suitcase.

I'd like to go on holiday to

....

....

In my suitcase, I'll take

....

....

I won't need

....

....

5 Can you guess where your friend would like to go? Ask and answer.

There are some trainers and an umbrella in my suitcase.

Are you going to Spain?

No, I'm going to England! I'm taking an umbrella because it rains.

Review 2

1 Write the words in the crossword.

Across →

4 I rode over a stone and now my bike has got a flat t........... .

5 We fed the ducks on the p........... .

6 I broke my watch and my dad r........... it.
Now it works again.

7 A bicycle has two. A car has four. They're w........... .

Down ↓

1 To cross the river you go over the b........... .

2 I've got a new bicycle. I go c........... on it every day after school.

3 I wear this on my head when I go cycling. It's a h........... .

6 I like travelling by train on the r........... .

2 Read and circle. Then match to the pictures.

1 My dad works in an office. He's a **businessman / businesswoman**.

2 I work in a very tall building. I work in a **meeting / skyscraper**.

3 I write about the news. I'm a **newspaper / journalist**.

4 My sister writes in her **meeting / diary** every day.

5 Can you put the letter in the **envelope / exit**, please?

6 My brother loves building robots. He wants to be an
engineer / entrance when he grows up.

3 Choose and write.

shelves   gym   history   geography   languages   dictionary   member   students   science

My School Day

Today my first lesson was English. I enjoyed it because I like learning ¹.*languages* .
After that I learnt about rivers and mountains in ²................ . Then in our ³................
lesson we learnt what life was like in Roman times. At lunchtime, lots of ⁴................ .
played outside. But I'm a ⁵................ of the book club, so I went to the library. There
are lots of ⁶................ in the library, full of books. I read a book in English, and when
I didn't know a word I used a ⁷................ . After lunch, I learnt about plants and
animals in my ⁸................ lesson. Then I went to the ⁹................ to play basketball
with my friends.

4 Complete the puzzle. Find the mystery word.

1 This is a place where birds sit on their eggs.

2 Some animals have spots on their fur or wings. They're …

3 This insect has bright colourful wings.

4 This kind of animal lives outside. It doesn't live with people.

5 This is a word that means animal.

6 This is a bird with a long, white neck.

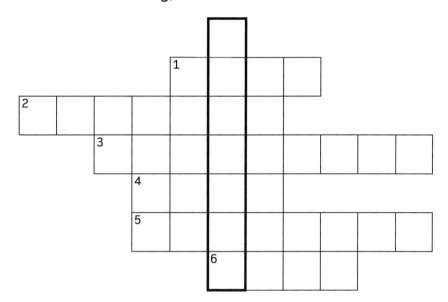

5 (R.1) Listen and circle. Which suitcase did Richard take on holiday?

1

2

Now complete the sentences.

Richard took a bottle of ¹............................... , and some ²............................... .
He took his favourite blue ³............................... . He took a green and white
spotted ⁴............................... , black ⁵............................... and a pair of red
⁶............................... .

Extra vocabulary

The seasons

1 (11.1) (11.2) Listen, point and say. Now listen and number.

spring   summer   autumn   winter

2 (11.3) Write the months. Then listen, point and say.

| September   April   February   June   ~~January~~ |

1	2	3	4
January	....	**March**	....
5	**6**	**7**	**8**
May	....	**July**	**August**
9	**10**	**11**	**12**
....	**October**	**November**	**December**

3 (11.4) Listen and say the month

4 Now close your book. Can you say all the months of the year?

5 What month is your birthday? Ask around the class.

> What month is your birthday?

> It's in February. How about you?

> My birthday is in July.